MW00445358

Anita the Alligator
FEELS ANGRY

Written by **John Wood**

Illustrated by **Danielle Jones**

BookLife
PUBLISHING

©2019
Book Life
King's Lynn, Norfolk PE30 4LS

ISBN: 978-1-78637-369-4

All rights reserved
Printed in Malaysia

A catalogue record for this book is available from the British Library.

Written by:
John Wood

Edited by:
Holly Duhig

Designed & Illustrated by:
Danielle Jones

With grateful thanks to Place2Be for their endorsement of this series.
These titles have been developed to support teachers and school counsellors in exploring pupils' mental health, and have been
reviewed and approved by the clinical team at Place2Be, the leading national children's mental health charity.

THINGS TO THINK ABOUT...

Here are some questions to think about while reading this book:

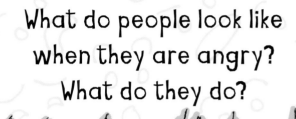

What do people look like when they are angry? What do they do?

Have you ever felt angry before? Do you feel like Anita when you are angry, or do you feel differently?

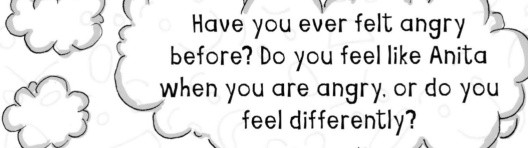

It is OK to be angry, but it is important not to break things or hurt other people. How would other people feel if we shouted at them or hurt them?

Anita the Alligator is staring at the **BIG** lump of mashed potato on her dinner plate. Anita doesn't like mashed potato.

NOT ONE BIT.

Anita's family are looking at a scan of the **new baby**.

"Will we have a little brother?"

asks Anita's sister, Millie.

Mum nods, smiling.

Anita is **SICK** of all the baby talk.

She leaves the table to get some juice but,

halfway to the fridge, she trips over

a *shiny* new pram.

Anita is hurt. She wants to **growl**

and her arms feel shaky.

Her heart goes
THUMP,
THUMP,
THUMP in her chest.

Anita has had enough!

"I do not want to eat any more," says Anita, suddenly.

"Finish your dinner, Anita," says Dad.

"I DON'T WANT TO!"

screams Anita.

She sticks her hand in her dinner
and throws it across the table!

Millie doesn't like it when Anita gets ANGRY.
When Anita gets ANGRY, it is like living with a MONSTER
who throws mashed potato at you.

There's potato on the chairs...

There's some in Millie's hair...

THERE'S MASHED POTATO EVERYWHERE!

"Don't worry,"

says Dad, as he hides under

the table with Mum.

"ANITA!" shouts Mum.

Anita turns to look at her mum.
Then she looks at the potato-covered room.
She didn't mean to get so carried away.

Mum decides to take Anita to her room to calm down.
It's much quieter there.

"Take some s l o w, **deep** breaths, Anita,"
says Mum.

"What's the matter?" asks Mum.

"I'm scared of the new baby. I don't want things to change," says Anita.

"I'm worried that you will love the baby instead of me."

Mum gives Anita a hug.
"Everything changes, Anita," says Mum.

"Well, almost everything.
Your family will always love you.
That will never change."

Dad and Millie peek through the door.
"Is it safe to come in?" asks Millie.

Mum tells Anita to go and help Millie
wash her hair in the bath.

"Sorry for throwing food
in your hair, Millie," says Anita, as they
go to the bathroom.

"That's OK," says Millie, as she holds Anita's hand.
"I'm just glad it wasn't fish pie night."

Later, Anita has a dream. She is having dinner with her family and there is a **very special guest.**

IT'S HER LITTLE BROTHER!

On the table there is a FEAST. There are sausages, beans, ice cream and chocolate cake. And there's not one bit of mashed potato in sight.

THINGS TO THINK ABOUT...

After reading this book, try answering these questions.

Why was Anita so angry?
Can you think of any other
reasons people get angry?

Anita takes deep breaths
when she feels angry.
Can you think of any other
ways to calm down?

Was Anita wrong to throw her food?
What should we say to people when
we do something wrong?